D0230593

WHEN MY MIND
WINDS UP

WHEN MY MIND WINDS UP

A PULL NO PUNCHES APPROACH TO ANXIETY

Jennifer Ervig

New Harbor Press

Copyright © 2019 Jennifer Ervig

All rights reserved. No part of this publication may be reproduced, distributed or transmitted in any form or by any means, including photocopying, recording, or other electronic or mechanical methods, without the prior written permission of the publisher, except in the case of brief quotations embodied in critical reviews and certain other non-commercial uses permitted by copyright law. For permission requests, write to the publisher, addressed "Attention: Permissions Coordinator," at the address below.

New Harbor Press
1601 Mt Rushmore Rd, Ste 3288
Rapid City, SD 57701
www.newharborpress.com

Ordering Information:
Quantity sales. Special discounts are available on quantity purchases by corporations, associations, and others. For details, contact the "Special Sales Department" at the address above.

When My Mind Winds Up/Ervig —1st ed.

ISBN 978-1-63357-212-6

First edition: 10 9 8 7 6 5 4 3 2 1

Scriptures taken from the Holy Bible, New International Version®, NIV®. Copyright © 1973, 1978, 1984, 2011 by Biblica, Inc.™ Used by permission of Zondervan. All rights reserved worldwide. www.zondervan.com The "NIV" and "New International Version" are trademarks registered in the United States Patent and Trademark Office by Biblica, Inc.™

Contents

Prologue 1

Consider Others Better Than Yourself: It's Not About You 3

Period Prozac 9

Perhaps if You Can't Trust God it's because You Don't Know Him 13

Stop Insulting God with Worry 17

Emergency Kit for When You're in the Pit 23

It's a Matter of Mind Over Matter................................27

Anxiety vs Depression 33

Look Good Feel Good..37

Pay it Forward..41

What Brings You Joy? 45

Happiness Versus Joy 49

Making the Joy of the Lord My Own............................55

Anxiety Makes Me Funny 61

Notes 63

Pray Before You Cray..65

Perspective Paves the Way to Healing..........................69

Devotions at Night Make for a Good Night's Sleep 75

As Iron Sharpens Iron 79

Doubt Your Doubts and Believe Your Beliefs 83

Hope That Anchors the Soul 87

Why Me? Well, Why Not? 91

Why Aren't *They* Anxious? 95

Tears Are Okay 99

Emotional Intelligence 103

Be Honest with Yourself and Others 107

Jesus Sweat Blood 111

Do it Afraid or Rather, Anxious 115

Hugs Not Drugs 119

All Kinds of Anxious 123

Today I'm Fine 127

How Do People Cope Without Jesus? 131

Stop
FIGHTING YOURSELF
&
Start
FIGHTING *for* YOURSELF

Prologue

F riends, I am no counselor, psychologist or psychiatrist. I am just a girl who has struggled with this thing called anxiety as long as I can remember. Also, I still don't have it all figured out. However, I'm a lot further on my journey to freedom from anxiety than I used to be, so I just wanna share what I've learned and what helps. Life is meant to be done with others and I think it's so important to share our struggles and strengths with each other in order to make their burdens a bit lighter and a little less lonely.

Additionally, I want to take a moment to thank my two illustrators, Anna Ahlbrecht and Hudson Baumgart. Anna did all the lettering in my graphics as well as edited the first draft of my manuscript. She's a woman of many talents. Now, Hudson; well, he's a doll. One day, I was in a meeting in his dad's office and he was drawing these cute little monsters on the white board. I fell in love with them as they represented little worry monsters to me. I just knew I needed them in my book! Worry can often appear as somewhat alluring, but we have to remember it's a monster and reject it.

Lastly, I want to offer a suggestion. I've often referred to anxiety as "my anxiety". A dear friend, Tammy Emineth, has scolded me every time I've done so. Words have power. Do not claim anxiety as your own. It's not meant for you. It's just anxiety - and it's on its way out. Amen?

Consider Others Better Than Yourself: It's Not About You

Introductory Thoughts: Let's just start this off real blunt: anxiety *can* be really selfish. This is true whether you can help your battle with anxiety or not. Does this fact make you feel even more hopeless? Probably, but it shouldn't. Once I figured this out, it was actually more freeing and a help I could pull out of my tool box again and again.

Read: Philippians 2:3

Anxiety is very self focusing. Your mind gets locked in a constant loop of "I suck", "Why did I do that?", "I'm such a moron", "No wonder so many people don't like me". See the pattern here? We have to grasp the rope of hope that says it's not about me and remember we're not always the cat's meow no matter what. Nobody is. Grab that - and let it reel you right on out of that dark pit. So, how do we do that? We refuse to stay in that thought pattern, humble ourselves, and esteem others as better.

Rebuke the Selfish Movie Reel

Correcting anxious thoughts can be exhausting. However, just like constantly redirecting, and being firm with a toddler is exhausting, putting in the around the clock effort now will pay off down the road.

When my kids were babies and tots I never moved breakables or plants. I never put guards on the entertainment system.

I simply taught them what they could and couldn't touch; what they did and didn't have access to. Was it infuriating? For the first few days when they entered their "touch everything stage" when cruising and walking, of course it was! However, I could take them to any friend's home and any store and didn't have to worry about a thing! Every Christmas I had a Christmas tree and after the first three "mom-looks" and "nuh-uhs" my tree was intact and beautiful. It was worth the initial constant effort!

The same is true for anxiety. Constantly rebuke and reject every negative thought. Refuse to give up and mope. Keep praying that you'll have your wits about you and a God perspective of reality. Every time you find yourself looking down at your feet, lift your head up and see what's out and ahead. Is it hard? Yes. And honestly, I wasn't mature or wise enough to finally put the work in on this until after decades of battling with and suffering from anxiety. But, once I did put the work in, it got easier and easier. It was as if I had slowly built myself a staircase out of my pit of despair so that every time I fell back in, all I had to do was climb the stairs. Of course, I still had to do the work of climbing the stairs, but the staircase was already built! Are you picking up what I'm puttin' down here, folks?

Take Yourself Down a Notch

Carey Nieuwhof, in his book Didn't See It Coming, says "Pain is selfish. Not convinced pain is selfish? Drop a concrete brick on your toe and see if you can focus on anything else." Did you respond the same way I did after reading that? It was an 'aha' moment for me! When we're in pain, depressed or anxious we don't realize that we're focused on ourselves because it's not like we're taking pleasure in it! The pain of anxiety is deceitful when it comes to being self focused.

But think about it. If we're constantly berating ourselves for being total idiots, completely unlovable, and giant screw ups, then we must've thought awfully high of ourselves in the first place, huh?

One big thing that would always trigger my anxiety is if I made a mistake. I'm such a perfectionist that if I ever made a blunder, I'd crucify myself over and over until one day God gently tapped me on the shoulder and said, "uh...hey, Jen, who made you queen of the universe, incapable of missing the mark?" In that moment, I apologized to God for acting like I should have been God and although I felt convicted, I no longer felt condemned.

Take Others Up a Notch

Ahh...the third ingredient to the solution for selfish anxiety trifecta - consider others better than yourself. Philippians 2:3 says "Let nothing *be done* through selfish ambition or conceit, but in lowliness of mind let each esteem others better than himself." The problem with anxiety is that we don't know we are doing it through selfish ambition or conceit until we're made aware by our own 'aha' moment. I hope this book does that for you. Once you reject the selfish movie reel and take yourself down a notch, you can keep yourself on the right track by considering others as better than you.

Does this mean they are better than you? No! God is no respecter of persons, but esteeming others as better is a healthy mindset for us all to have. It keeps our own hearts and minds in check. It examines our motives and mindsets. It removes our natural instinct to have a god complex.

If my world is swirling out of control around me and everything is doom and gloom because I'm such a loser, how freeing it is to tell myself "So what! I'm nothing special. Many people better than me have it a lot worse off." Bam! Perspective shift. Downward spiral stopped in its tracks. Merry Go Round has finally stopped and I can step or crawl off a little dizzy, unsure and unbalanced but safe and sound nonetheless.

So, there you have it. Anxiety is not *about* you. It's an attack *on* you. Satan loves to lie and not only make us think it's about us, but keep us locked in that selfish loop unawares. Break free. Build the staircase out of the pit. Remember you're not all that and a bag of chips. In fact, you're usually only the bag of chips; and that's okay. Phew, pressure is off; you're not the main attraction, but being the bag of chips provides that saltiness everyone craves. ;)

Jen says own it and make it real:

What is one thing you can do today to apply what you've just read to your life? Rebuke negative thoughts and start building your staircase? If so, how? Repenting for being self focused? If so, what does that look like? Take time to pray and journal about it now.

Anxiety

IS NOT ABOUT YOU.

It's an attack on you.

SATAN LOVES TO *lie* AND NOT ONLY MAKE US THINK IT'S ABOUT US, BUT KEEP US LOCKED IN THAT SELFISH LOOP *unawares*.

Notes

_____

_____

_____

_____

_____

_____

_____

_____

_____

_____

_____

_____

Period Prozac

Introductory Thoughts: There's a negative stigma around taking prescriptions for anxiety. It seems to be especially so in the church and I don't know why. I feel like God gave us these things to help so why not use them? Of course, the caution is to be sure we're using them as an aid and not as the answer.

Read: Jeremiah 8:22; Revelation 22:2; Isaiah 38:21

Sometimes no matter how much you try to take your thoughts captive or how hard you try to hold onto your joy, you could use a little boost. It's at those times that medical help, including medications, may be a good idea. The decision to use such help is definitely between you and God (and your doctor) so use wisdom and involve God in the whole process.

That being said, I'd like you to remember the difference between conviction and condemnation. Conviction leaves you with a feeling of caution but fills you with hope and retains your joy. Condemnation fills you with dread and guilt, and makes you feel hopeless. Why do I bring this up? Because if you're feeling condemned about taking medical help, just boot that to the curb and you do you, boo.

TMI Confession

I use a generic version of Prozac, but only 3 days before my period, through my period, and until three days after my period.

Why? Because my hormones actually feed a lot into my depression and anxiety. PMS is a little beyond normal for me.

I remember in my teen years my mom mentioning that I may need my hormones checked or something but of course as a teen I thought she was just being mean. Then, I got married. Haha... my husband oddly noticed the same thing as my mom. Imagine that! So, I went to the doc. My doctor happens to be an amazing, funny, God-fearing man, by the way. I got lucky. He mentioned that hormone testing and all that's involved with that is crazy expensive so he suggested the period Prozac. It's so seldom used the way I use it that even the pharmacist was like "Wow. I've never seen this before." But, you know, it works for me. It takes the edge off.

Most of the time, I have an okay grip on my battle with anxiety, but when shark week rolls around and Aunt Flo comes to stay, I need to call in reinforcements. And you know what? That's okay. I have a friend, Sami, who says "all I need is Prozac and Jesus". #dreamteam, am I right? Haha!

Anxiety can be physical, mental, emotional and spiritual. Your anxiety could be caused by one or a combination of those factors; and it's different for everyone. Therefore, I do believe some people need the help of medicine. If you feel the conviction that you do without the condemnation for doing so, go for it. Additionally, if you feel the conviction that you shouldn't, heed that as well.

Of course, it's a balance. I wouldn't ever want to become so dependent on my meds that my brain is so fogged I can't even think to take my thoughts captive and worship Jesus, and in the process lose the spark that's my personality. I also wouldn't want to feel like I'm fighting a losing battle trying to retain joy and direct my thoughts. Therefore, my low dose of period Prozac just when I need it every month works for me. For now, I have that perfect balance. I pray that you feel you do too.

Jen says own it and make it real:

Do you take medications to help with depression and anxiety? If so, how do you feel about that? If you don't, do you think you need to? If so, how do you feel about that? Whatever your answers are, take them to God and to someone you trust and talk it out.

Notes

_____

_____

_____

_____

_____

_____

_____

_____

_____

_____

_____

_____

Perhaps if You Can't Trust God it's because You Don't Know Him

Introductory Thoughts: I have a photo of a flower hanging on my fridge and on it, it says:

"'We only trust people we know', says Martha Tennison, a popular women's conference speaker. If you're struggling to trust God, it may be because you don't know God."

Whoa! That hits me right in the feels, ya know? I received this as a take home item from some women's event and it's been on my fridge ever since, because it holds a power packed truth filled punch that I'd be wise to not soon forget.

Read: Proverbs 3:5; Psalm 46:10; Psalm 9:10; Isaiah 26:3 (*pssst... these are great for memorizing*)

We only trust people we know. On the other hand, sometimes *because* we know people, we don't trust them! I think that's one of the reasons the quote on my fridge stands out to me. I *know* God! He has never let me down! Not even once! Even when I thought He was letting me down, it's only because I'm finite and I didn't know the full picture. When I let God lead, things always turn out better for me (and those I love). So, why on earth would I let worry reign in my heart and mind, taking over the place of confident trust and faith that my Savior holds me and my whole world in His capable hands?

I think the answer is clear. When you stop spending ample time with people, you begin to forget or take for granted all the special things about them. Think about it. When you finally see a girlfriend you haven't spent time with in years, you think to yourself as you're both drinking coffee in your favorite shop, "Ah man, I forgot how contagious her laugh is". When you haven't had your mom's casserole in a long time, you savor it and remember how comforting it is to eat her cooking. When you're cleaning out a closet and you find an old box full of past birthday cards, you read them and remember what dear friends you've been blessed with. All it takes to reignite these memories is CONTACT.

Spend time with your Jesus. Ask the Holy Spirit to remind you of all He's done for you. Read His word and see how He's come through for His people time and again. Pray to Him and pour out your heart and see if He would ever abuse the privilege of being the one you run to. He would not. He has not.

Jen says own it and make it real:
Where have you been struggling to trust God? How does it make you feel to learn your distrust is maybe due to not knowing Him? How can you personally cultivate trust in God?

Notes

_____

_____

_____

_____

_____

_____

_____

_____

_____

_____

_____

_____

Stop Insulting God with Worry

Introductory Thoughts: Every time I worry, I tell God I don't trust Him. That's gotta cut deep and for that, I'm sorry. Lord, please forgive me for offending you with my worry. Help me in my unbelief.

Read: Phillippians 4:6-7; Hebrews 11:1; Matthew 6

I know what you're thinking. I know because I've thought it too. You're thinking worry is not an insult; it simply shows that you care. That thought is what we call a wolf in sheep's clothing. Satan's lies always include some truth. Of course you care! That is a big reason WHY you worry! However, the truth remains that it's kind of a slap in God's beautiful face.

Three Big Insults:
When I worry about mistakes of the past, I'm saying that I'm not sure if God really forgives or loves me. According to the Enneagram (check out the book The Road Back to You) I'm a 1 with a wing of 2. That 2 in me believes that I'm loved for what I do. That 1 in me believes rules are law and there's no straying. Therefore, if I mess up, I berate myself to no end and the whole world comes crashing down. Obviously, I ain't gettin' into heaven. How do you think that makes God feel? He laid down His life for the JOY set before Him and I *doubt* that? I really think my mistakes are such a big deal that they can negate the majesty, wonder and beauty of the greatest moment in the history of all mankind? Yikes.

When I worry about what's happening in the present, I am proclaiming that I'm not sure if God is in control. Psalms 95:4 tells us that in His hands are the depths of the earth and the mountain tops belong to Him. It reminds me of a song from childhood called "He's Got the Whole World in His Hands". He literally holds us! I think that puts Him in control.

And when I worry about the future, I'm admitting that I'm not sure if God will take care of me. Let's just read the following, shall we?

> *Matthew 6:25-34 New International Version (NIV)*
> *25 "Therefore I tell you, do not worry about your life, what you will eat or drink; or about your body, what you will wear. Is not life more than food, and the body more than clothes? 26 Look at the birds of the air; they do not sow or reap or store away in barns, and yet your heavenly Father feeds them. Are you not much more valuable than they? 27 Can any one of you by worrying add a single hour to your life?*
> *28 "And why do you worry about clothes? See how the flowers of the field grow. They do not labor or spin. 29 Yet I tell you that not even Solomon in all his splendor was dressed like one of these. 30 If that is how God clothes the grass of the field, which is here today and tomorrow is thrown into the fire, will he not much more clothe you—you of little faith? 31 So do not worry, saying, 'What shall we eat?' or 'What shall we drink?' or 'What shall we wear?' 32 For the pagans run after all these things, and your heavenly Father knows that you need them. 33 But seek first his kingdom and his righteousness, and all these things will be given to you as well. 34 Therefore do not worry about tomorrow, for tomorrow will worry about itself. Each day has enough trouble of its own.*

My favorite part of that is verse 33, because it says if you seek Him first, the rest will be added to you. Up above it mentions that *not even* Solomon in all his splendor was dressed like the birds! If you know the story of Solomon, you know that because he sought God's ways and asked for wisdom, God did indeed give him all the splendor of the world as well! We've seen God come through on this promise before. Let's not worry. Let's not doubt. Let's seek Him, receive and rest secure about the future. Sound good?

No more questioning who God is. When my faith is shaky, I keep trying to have faith in myself or in who knows what - and THAT, my friends, adds a whole lotta gas to the fire of anxiety!

Hebrews 11:1 is my favorite verse. It says, "faith is being sure of what you hope for and certain of what you don't see". I am sure of God. I'm sure of who He is and what He's capable of even if my eyes deceive me.

Jen says own it and make it real:
Why is worry an insult to God? How does it make you feel to think you may have insulted God? How do you make an effort to trust God?

Notes

_____

_____

_____

_____

_____

_____

_____

_____

_____

_____

_____

_____

LORD, please forgive me FOR OFFENDING YOU WITH my worry HELP ME WITH my unbelief

Emergency Kit for When You're in the Pit

Introductory Thoughts: Are you ever just so lost in despair that you wish someone would just tell you what to do? Consider this chapter your go-to list when you can't think straight. You're welcome!

Read: Hebrews 6:10; Galatians 5:13; 1 Peter 4:10; James 5:16; 2 Peter 1:4

When I was 20, I was engaged to be married and it all blew up about a month before the wedding. My whole life's goal since a teenager was to be married and have kids, so to be this close to having that dream realized and then have it all fall apart was just devastating. I went into a serious deep depression.

During these dark times, I learned something that I didn't expect. I learned that if I focus on other people, joy comes flooding in. Remember; I've said that pain is selfish. It's selfish because we can't help but focus on how *we're* feeling, and how *we're* wronged, and how *we're* desperate. However, when we lift up our eyes and look outward, we gain a new outlook.

I found solace in helping clean the house where I was living. It brought me such joy to know that I could help make someone else's life so much better by just taking part in chores. Then, suddenly...for a while at least, I forgot how bleak my life was! It was intoxicating and I wanted to hold onto that feeling. Some people go to substance addictions to "escape". I escaped through service addiction!

As I continued to grow and mature through the years, I expanded on that realization. Every time I got incredibly blue, I'd:

- Look for someone to serve, yes but also;
- Pray for the joy, peace, health and good fortune of someone else;
- Read the Bible and claim God's promises in my life

Praying for Others:
Have you ever heard someone say that what they're going through is so bad, they wouldn't wish it on anyone? Have *you* said that? Well, then let's get practical about it and mean it by not only not wishing it on anyone but praying against it!

Ever since that break up with my fiancé happened to me, I've prayed earnestly for those whose dream it is to be married. I've prayed that people would have the right partners and that they would never experience what I went through.

When you feel blue, pray for someone. We're not alone on this planet. Everyone goes through dark times. Praying for others helps you remember that and it's a quick pick me up.

Reading the Bible:
I'm sure this last one seems obvious but when you're in dark despair, your brain doesn't work right and the obvious eludes you. But, seriously, people. Read your Bible. Read the Psalms and connect with the heartache expressed. Read Phillippians and hold onto your joy because you know that there's more to life than what you're going through. Read all about your identity in Christ and all the promises that have been claimed over you and repeat them to yourself and in prayer over and over again.

I know the dark places suck. I get it. I've been there, but being "others focused" by praying for them and serving them while you connect with God's word sure brings a whole lot of joy in the morning. It sure releases a whole lot of pain. It sure brings a whole lot of healing. When you're busy looking out for others, it's impossible to stay in your own head. It simply can't be done. This emergency kit to pull you out of the pit is a fail safe that works Every. Single. Time. It's quick and easy freedom *and* it's addictive.

Jen says own it and make it real:
Why would serving others help you when you're feeling desperate and lost? How do you feel about the fact that I liken it to a type of addiction to escape? What would you add to this emergency kit to escape?

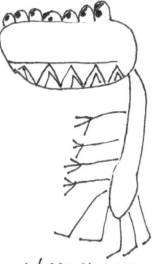

WORRY MONSTER

Notes

_____

_____

_____

_____

_____

_____

_____

_____

_____

_____

_____

It's a Matter of Mind Over Matter

Introductory Thoughts: Sure. There are horrible things in your life that are absolutely true. They're fact. They're reality. However, the thoughts that accompany them can be absolutely false, keeping those horrific things in your life alive and well.

Read: Phillippians 4:8; 2 Corinthians 10:5; 2 Timothy 1:7 (*memorize these!*)

The power of the mind is unreal. The power of the mind literally boggles my mind! Our thoughts rule so much of our worlds. I found a quote by some dude named Earl Nightingale that says, "Whatever we plant in our subconscious mind and nourish with repetition and emotion will one day become reality". DUH! Yet, we always forget. Why? Because we are too busy planting and nourishing anything other than the truth. We stand there pointing non stop at the horror in our hearts and minds heralding its existence. "Look what's here! Can you believe it?", we wail. So, it keeps standing tall and proud, claiming its territory, sinking its roots in deep. Stop planting and nourishing lies. Just pluck them little buggers outta your brain and start a burn pile!

How to Weed out 'Dem Buggers:
I don't know how you weed your garden, but a popular approach is to pull them as soon as you see them. Walking out on your

porch to grab that Amazon package before your spouse sees it and notice the intruder in your pansy pot? Pull it. This is the approach I try to take with my thought weeds.

The problem arises when the weed is attractive. Let's face it; some weeds are kinda pretty. In fact, some people let dandelions run rampant in their yards because they find them so appealing! Sometimes my thoughts, weedy buggers that they are, are kinda entertaining. They're kinda intriguing. It's like a freak show or horrific accident that you can't look away from. So you sit there, a captive audience just waiting to see what *might* happen. You know it's not *right* but you can't look away...not yet anyway. Maybe these thoughts are:

- Self harm
- Suicide
- Creating drama
- Leaving your family
- Fantasizing about someone's doom
- Imagining worst case scenarios
- Contemplating sin
- BELIEVING LIES

So, you sit there intrigued while these thought weeds start to multiply. Then, all of a sudden, you're overwhelmed by them. They're killing your favorite plants near them and it takes a lot more work to get rid of them once you finally realize they're more trouble than they're worth. Ahhhhh! Best to shut them down at the get go. Best to "take them captive and make them submit".

Nourishing the Good Stuff:
Weeds, left to their own devices, take over. However, just like anything good in life, the plants we *want* to keep need attention and nourishment to thrive. The good stuff takes work. The true, noble, right, pure, lovely, admirable, excellent and praiseworthy

stuff needs nourishment and all your attention! Feed them with your attention and things like Bible reading and prayer. Purposely plant more of them so there's no room for weed thoughts! Admire and appreciate them often!

Remember, no matter what is real in your life, it's all a matter of mind over matter. Yeah...

- Your kid may be sick
- You may not be able to pay your bills
- Your friend may not be talking to you
- Lies may appear so very true
- Your world may literally be crumbling around you

BUT...

What IS true right now? What's admirable? What's praiseworthy in the midst of all of this? Yes, life can suck, but the Life Giver brings hope and a promise...of a new reality! Feed the hope. Focus on that promise of a better future! Mind over matter, people...every time.

Jen says own it and make it real:
What kind of weeds have you left to their own devices in your mind? What are the good things in your life you miss because those weed thoughts are choking them out? What are you gonna do about it? What did you buy off Amazon lately that you're hiding from your spouse? (Haha...that last one was a trick...but seriously, go check the porch before they see it. You're welcome.)

Notes

_____

_____

_____

_____

_____

_____

_____

_____

_____

_____

_____

Stop PLANTING & NOURISHING lies.

Anxiety vs Depression

Introductory Thoughts: Okay, so I'm mostly anxious. I'm a worrier at heart, but occasionally I get so distraught over my ridiculous anxiousness that I can move into a depression and basically chalk everything up to pointless. I get to these points where I'm like "why be so frazzled and worried? It's useless energy. Might as well resign to the fact, that you're always gonna be this way."

Read: 2 Timothy 1:7; Deuteronomy 31:8; Psalms 34:17 (*psst... memorize these too*)

So how are anxiety and depression alike or different anyway? According to psycom.net, common depression symptoms may be:

- depressed mood
- lack of interest in enjoyable activities
- increase or decrease in appetite
- insomnia or hypersomnia
- slowing of movement
- lack of energy
- feelings of guilt or worthlessness
- trouble concentrating
- suicidal thoughts or behaviors.

And anxiety symptoms may look like:

- excessive worry
- restlessness
- being easily fatigued
- trouble concentrating
- irritability
- sleep disturbance
- muscle tension

While there's some overlap on both lists such as fatigue, insomnia and trouble concentrating, there's definite differences as well. Depressed individuals usually move slowly and they appear as if the "spark or light" has gone out of life. Anxious individuals, however, can't seem to calm down; they're basically in some form of panic mode. Depressed people don't seem to care about much, whereas anxious people are concerned about even the most ridiculous of things!

If you're not sure if you have anxiety or depression or both, I encourage you to see your doctor and find out. Read about both. Ask your family and those closest to you what they notice. Pray for answers and wisdom. Taking these steps are important because self awareness leads to clarity and health. God's plan for you is to have joy and a sound mind. Figure out where you're at now, so you can make your way to His perfect plan for your life.

Jen says own it and make it real:
Do you think you're anxious, depressed or both? Why do you think that? How does knowing the differences and similarities between them help you? What are some practical next steps you can take to help you achieve greater clarity for your situation?

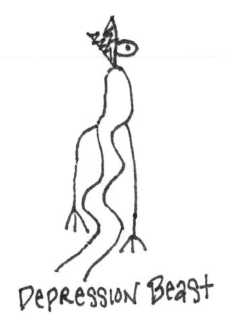

Depression Beast

Notes

_____

_____

_____

_____

_____

_____

_____

_____

_____

_____

_____

Look Good Feel Good

Introductory Thoughts: Okay, so this may seem really shallow to some of you, but there's an undeniable truth to it that truly helps me in a simple and practical way. When I think I look good, I feel good. Plain and simple. When you take extra care of yourself, it shows you care about yourself. And, yes, for you guys reading this book this is kind of a girly entry, but hang in there with me.

Read: Ephesians 5:29; Psalms 139:14; Matthew 15:11

There are two things I do to take pride in my appearance that help keep anxiety and the blues at bay:
I keep my nails painted 90% of the time.
I buy the occasional new item for my wardrobe

Keeping My Nails Done:
As someone who deals with anxiety and depression on the regular, somehow having my digits dutifully cutiful helps a little. And I am dutiful about it. I paint them myself every Friday night. Okay, sometimes Thursday or Saturday, but pretty regularly every Friday night.

(Ladies, because I know you're gonna ask, I use Sally Hansen products. They last the week without chipping. I use the quick dry top coat due to impatience to wait for them to dry.)

Having my nails done makes me feel put together, and if I'm put together, then I must not be as much of the complete wreck that I think I am. It's kinda that same feeling when your underwear matches your outfit...you just feel like you've got your stuff together and can conquer the day!

Additionally, I get compliments on my nails ALL. THE. TIME, and people ask me where I go to get them done. This lifts my spirit and strokes my ego because compliments are always nice mood boosters and...as you already know, I do them myself!

I asked my 14 year old son what the male version of painting nails might be and he says it's different for all guys (duh - stinkin' wise teen) but he likes to keep his kicks clean and his hair tight. So, we all got our thing. There you go, guys. See, this one was for you too.

Buying that New Wardrobe Piece

Okay, so this one can get unhealthy fast, but yeah, I shop when I'm blue...in MODERATION! Don't you dare worry, my husband keeps me in check on this one. GAH! The reason stress shopping and stress eating are bad is because they spiral out of control fast. However, the reason they were ever ideas in the first place is because, kept simple, it's a nice little mood booster.

The Trick to it All?

The trick to making these little look good feel good tricks work for you is this:

Keep the Main thing the Main thing

Use this chapter in conjunction with the others. God is the source of your joy. God is the source of your identity. Don't believe the lie that how you look depicts what is inside. Don't believe the lie that comfort and peace comes from candy apple red polish and a leather bomber. Do take your hubby or girlfriend shopping with you to keep you in check. Do allow your hubby or girlfriend to pour truth into you as you scroll Amazon and Poshmark. Do let the happy little colors on your nails depict that you take pride in who God made you; not that you're trying to hide what you're ashamed of. The look good feel good method is an embellishment and a mood booster, not a cover up.

Jen says own it and make it real:
Why does taking pride in how we look boost our moods? The next time you wake up worried or blue, I encourage you to shower, put on the best looking, most confidence boosting thing you own, take a selfie and tag me in it with the hashtag #lookgood-feelgood. I'll pray for ya and, barring being bombarded with such posts, compliment ya too. Deal?

Notes

_____

_____

_____

_____

_____

_____

_____

_____

_____

_____

_____

Pay it Forward

Introductory Thoughts: Have you seen the movie Pay it Forward? It came out in 2000. The movie tells the story of a social studies teacher who gives a class assignment to think of an idea to change the world for the better, then put it into action. One amazing young man in that junior high class creates a plan for "paying forward" favors. Not only does he affect the life of his struggling single mom, but he sets in motion an unprecedented wave of human kindness which, unbeknownst to him, has bloomed into an amazing national phenomenon. If you haven't seen it, I highly suggest you do. If you're feeling blue, it will give you the warm and fuzzies.

Read: Matthew 7:12

The reason I bring up the movie is because the idea of paying it forward can really help us when we're struggling with anxiety and depression as well. As mentioned before, there's just something about forcing ourselves to be "others focused" that helps us get our minds out of our own woes - huh, imagine that!

What helps you when you're down or freaking out?
So what is it that you wish others would do for you when you're down in the dumps or so hopped up with worry you can't get back to reality? So many people don't help us when we're anxious or depressed because they simply don't know what to do. Since we're the experts, let's start doing for others what we know we'd like done for us. That simple act can change the whole tra-

jectory on how to help loved ones through these hard times. Not only that, but serving others in this way will keep us healthier on our own journey with the same battles.

Do you just need a friend to sit with you in silence? Be that friend for someone else! Do you wish others would not give advice? Don't give your advice either! Do you wish people would validate you when you do share? Do the same...say things like "Thanks for sharing that with me" or "Thanks for trusting me with your story".

We certainly know what doesn't help

Let's not avoid others. We know how that can feel. Let's not try to placate others and tell them to toughen up. Of course, we know it will, but we also know it doesn't feel like that in the moment. Let's not assume their problem will simply go away. Finally, let's definitely not make them feel that they're weak individuals or a burden on others.

When someone is in your world hopped up and anxious or deep in the dumps, pay the help forward. Do for them what has helped you in the past or what you wish others would do for you. It'll come back full circle. I promise.

Jen says own it and make it real:

So, what are some things that help you when you're struggling? How can you use that to help someone else?

Notes

_____

_____

_____

_____

_____

_____

_____

_____

_____

_____

_____

_____

What Brings You Joy?

Introductory Thoughts: I know that Marie Kondo says "Get rid of everything that doesn't spark joy", but that seems a little negative to me. How about we instead focus on what does bring joy?

Read: Proverbs 17:22; Psalms 94:19; Romans 15:13; Philemon 1:7; Romans 14:17

So, what brings you joy? Not happiness, mind you, but actual joy. Oh, I suppose I should attempt to define each in order to make myself quite clear. How's this?

Happiness is an emotion or a mood, but joy is an attitude.

That probably completely makes it worse, doesn't it? Let me try again. It's my belief that happiness is fickle, as it's based on circumstances. Joy, however, gets its source in Christ. It is both a gift from God available to everyone as well as a fruit of the Spirit that grows as we mature in Christ.

Therefore, what brings you joy? Actual joy? Is it seeing your family and friends happy and healthy? Is it seeing new believers commit their lives to Christ? Is it knowing your hope for a future with God in eternity is sure and real? Is it when you're firing on all cylinders in your giftings for whatever you're passionate about? What brings you joy?

I could say sugar cookies bring me joy, but that's really just happiness. I could say shopping brings me joy but that too is circumstantial...the moment I have to try on pants or swimwear, all joy is lost. So, what brings you joy?

Joy comes from a hope of something valuable and real. Joy does not derive from fleeting pleasures. So, I'll ask again. What brings you joy?

Jen says own it and make it real:
Why would I ask what brings you joy? Why do I want you to focus on that? What's on your happy list versus your joy list? Is there anything that is on both lists?

Notes

Happiness Versus Joy

Introductory Thoughts: As I type this right now, I am actually all prepared to speak at a conference about this very thing in about two weeks. The conference is a part of the Restore Movement. They're all about helping women heal (sorry guys) and you should really check them out at *therestoremovement.com*. In the meantime, I'm gonna try not to straight up copy/paste my sermon here (you'll never know, haha).

Read: Galatians 5:22-23; Psalms 19:8

Joy is something we obviously all want. Yet, I think most of us don't really understand what it is and therefore don't have a clue how to get it. In my search to define joy, I noticed something...I've noticed that the most joyful people have seen and gone through some of the worst this world has to offer. Not only that, but though they never would have asked for their life experiences and the way things worked out, they will tell you:

- They're glad they went through it
- They like who they are now *better*
- That life now is often *sweeter*

What the heck (oops, Christian swear word. Sorry!) is wrong with these people?!

For these ladies, joy is a fruit. Not an emotion. Joy is a fruit they grew through obedience. For the rest of us, joy is something we all long for but seems completely elusive. How come after laughing with friends, we sometimes go home and cry at night?

Why is it that after watching a comedy show, later when all is quiet, we feel sad? How come after receiving recognition, a job promotion or a marriage proposal, we still have the potential to feel empty? Those are all good things that are supposed to be the source of a happy life!

Why do people who have gone through abuse, rejection and worse seem to have joy figured out? What's the secret?

Joy is a fruit that grows through obedience. It's not an emotion or a mood but an attitude. It's a theologically grounded command that originates in Christ. So, when you hear Paul say "Rejoice in the Lord always; I say it again, rejoice", you don't have to despair that you can't force yourself to feel a certain way. You just have to obey what you know God wants you to do and remain others-focused so that the fruit of joy will begin to grow.

And the good news is that Joy **is** for all of us. It's a fruit of the Holy Spirit produced by God's work in us. People who have gone through tough stuff, but who have let Jesus in, respond to Him with love and obedience, ultimately producing Christ-originated joy. Happiness is merely an emotion, but **Joy is a fruit that grows through obedience**.

Everyone is so focused on being happy, but I'm telling you God doesn't care about your happiness if your joy is at stake! This is so backwards from what the world tells us. We often think I'll be happy "if only", when we should focus on being joyful "in spite of".

Happiness is circumstantial, but joy comes from God. When we obey, we're pruned and fertilized. How do you grow fruit? How do you grow anything? You prune it. You add fertilizer. That's how fruit grows. That's when deep joy is found. You grow through the hard stuff (pruning) and the stinky stuff (fertilizer). You don't get rid of it. You embrace the challenge of it. I know that's hard to hear when we're talking about the evil things that can happen in this world, but stay with me.

Something tells me that those who experience deep joy don't run from what ails them, but may even lean into it while keeping their focus on Christ.

The fruit of joy grows when we are aware of God's grace and relish his favor through obedience. How do we obey Him? We focus on him rather than difficulties that try to rob us of contentment. We focus on others that need Him. We do what he calls us to no matter what's happening around us and within us.

Being "joyful in spite of" does NOT mean we deny our discontent or stuff down negative emotions, BUT we throw it at the feet of Jesus! We bluntly tell him what ails us but then we remember who he is and are joyful **in** him (as a part of him). You see this played out constantly in the Psalms. Write these down to read later: Psalms 3, 13, 18, 43 and 103.

Joy is a fruit that grows through obedience. Now let me tell you about one person who experienced the worst but has more joy than anyone who ever lived. Nope...that's the next chapter! Stay tuned!

Jen says own it and make it real:
What is the difference between happiness and joy? Who are the most joyful people you know? What do you think makes them that way? Would you consider yourself joyful?

GOD DOESN'T CARE
ABOUT YOUR

happiness

WHEN YOUR

joy

IS AT STAKE.

Notes

_____

_____

_____

_____

_____

_____

_____

_____

_____

_____

_____

_____

Making the Joy of the Lord My Own

Introductory Thoughts: I know. I'm so mean. I short stopped ya on the last chapter, but it's only because there was so much content, I needed two chapters. Previously, we learned about the difference between happiness and joy and even a little about how to get that joy. Now, I'm gonna tell you more about obtaining that joy...and how it's not only your joy you'll get but the joy of the Lord himself! Wowza!

Read: Hebrews 12:12; John 15

Jesus. Jesus is the person who has experienced the worst the world has to offer yet has more joy than anyone ever has or ever could!

Hebrews 12:12 talks about the joy that Jesus had that sustained him through suffering. It says, "looking to Jesus, the founder and perfecter of our faith, who for the joy that was set before him endured the cross, despising the shame, and is seated at the right hand of the throne of God."

Now let me explain to you what I believe Jesus was experiencing on the cross. If you've seen The Passion of the Christ, you're very aware of the physical pain he endured: lashings, that thorny tiara, dragging up his heavy cross...ALL. THE. THINGS. But, let me share what else I believe He was going through.

You know that feeling of yuck you get inside when you've really messed up and you're just disgusted with yourself? That self loathing you feel when you've hurt someone? That worthless-ness you feel when you feel hopeless beyond all repair? I wonder if when Jesus was on that cross *PHYSICALLY DYING*, that he felt that too...for every person that ever was or ever will be. Let. That.Sink.In. And *not only* that but I also wonder if that the pain, agony and heartache that anyone has ever felt or ever will feel when they were or are being sexually abused, lied to, abandoned, beaten, tortured, starved, mocked, anyone who's been a victim of sin - I wonder if he also felt that pain for every person that was or ever will be. I also wonder if he mourned for all the evil things that were done with glee for every person that ever com-mitted evil things or ever will. Why? Because Paul tells us that God made him sin who knew no sin. This man who never did one thing wrong in his life took that punishment on for all of us, both the victims of sin and the perpetrators.....for the joy set before him! The what now? The joy set before him!

THAT - **THAT is what** he endured, put up with, pushed his way through, leaned into...all the while despising its shame FOR THE JOY SET BEFORE HIM...the joy that his Father would be pleased; would be proud, just like Hebrews says. The joy that he would set us all FREE from bondage, the joy that death would lose its sting, the joy that with him you and I would spend all eternity in perfect communion...a never ending celebration... never to cry, or hurt or cower again. THAT joy set before him.

John tells us in chapter 15 that, Jesus said to abide in him and obey him. Be a part of him and do what he says. "As the Father has loved me, so have I loved you. Now remain in my love. If you keep my commands (remember the previous chapter said joy grows through obedience), you will remain in my love, just as I have kept my Father's commands and remain in his love. I have told you this so that my joy may remain in you and that your joy may be complete." Did you catch that? Not only will we have our joy, but we'll have HIS, making our joy truly complete.

Joy is a fruit that grows through obedience. Joy is the good stuff. Happiness is a cheap imitation. Joy costs MUCH. You have to pay the price of pruning. The price of fertilizing. The price of obedience. But never will an investment reap such a high return. I am not saying that God means for terrible things to happen to us. They happen because of human free will in a broken world. What I'm saying is he, being the good Father that he is, doesn't let it end there. He uses what was meant for evil for good. He uses it to prune and fertilize our eventual crop of JOYFUL fruit.

Imagine if we all despised the shame of what we were enduring for the joy set before us! What would it look like if we relentlessly obeyed what we knew God wanted of us despite our circumstances? What if we all adopted a mindset of "having joy in spite of", rather than "I could be happy if only"?

Joy is a fruit that grows through obedience. What step are you going to take to acquire that joy today?

Jen says own it and make it real:
So, what step are you going to take? How did it strike you when I shared what I believe Jesus was really going through on the cross? How can having HIS joy help us in our battle with depression and anxiety?

Joy Thief

Notes

_____

_____

_____

_____

_____

_____

_____

_____

_____

_____

_____

_____

Anxiety Makes Me Funny

Introductory Thoughts: Have you seen the memes that say "My family is just dysfunctional enough to make me funny", or "I plan to love you and care for you and offer you just enough dysfunction to make you funny"? They crack me up because it's so very true. Dysfunction makes us funny...and sometimes there's nothing more dysfunctional than anxiety.

Read: Genesis 5:20; Romans 8:37; Proverbs 17:22

Look at many of the great comedians who seem to have suffered from depression, anxiety or both: Robin Williams, Chonda Pierce, Wayne Brady, Woody Allen, Drew Carey...the list goes on. There's something about the hard things in life that bring out humor. To cope? Maybe? Probably.

I know for me, when I'm uncomfortable or embarrassed, I'll crack a joke. Maybe it's a defense mechanism. People tell me I'm hilarious. They think I'm confident and an extrovert. They're often surprised to hear I suffer from anxiety and actually classify myself as an ambivert. When I'm silly, it's not always because I'm anxious or uncomfortable. Sometimes I'm truly just trying to make another person laugh because I love to do it.

However, I do think that those of us who are funny are often funny because we use the ailments and mishaps in life to be relatable through humor. When we make the tough things in life funny, they're no longer so tough. Ya feel?

In addition to that, I also think humor helps us process that hard stuff in life. It helps us put it into perspective and make light of it so that our hearts stay merry and light.

I kinda appreciate that about myself. If I'm gonna be an anxious wreck at least I'm funny! Laughter is good like a medicine.

Jen says own it and make it real:
Are you funny? Where do you think your humor comes from? How does humor ease the tension in the world? Do you consider humor something to hide behind or a way to heal? Why?

Notes

Pray Before You Cray

I ntroductory Thoughts: Pray all day. What?! It's really that simple.

Read: 1 Thessalonians 5:16-18

I was going to tell you to pray when you feel yourself going crazy, but that's just stupid. We all know it doesn't work like that. Rather, I'm going to tell you to pray all day. That way, you'll always be prayin' before you cray.

The time in my life I felt closest to the Lord was when I was around 19 or 20. I vividly remember being shift lead and the teacher of the one year old toddler class at a daycare and pre-school. I LITERALLY talked to God all day long. I often worried that I may look crazy to others because although most conversations were in my head, sometimes my lips moved or my lightly breathed words became audible.

I literally prayed over each child during their diaper change. I lifted up every random thought that went through my head up to the Lord. I made myself constantly aware of his presence. Like, no joke, if I saw a pretty flower I'd be all "Lord, great job with that one". If a child in my class did something to make me laugh, I'd say "God, that was hilarious. Thanks for that". If I ate something gross, I'd be like "God, seriously. I thought you liked me". Haha! But this is for real. I was in constant, unending dialogue with Him over every stupid little thing. We were best friends.

In addition to that, at my lunch hour, I made sure to read four chapters of the Bible before eating. That was the first time I'd ever read the whole Bible all the way through! When I was at home, I also made sure to spend time praying or worshipping before I did anything fun like watching T.V.

This was one of the only times (or at least the longest period) of my life that I didn't feel regularly consumed with fear or worry. Life was easy(ish). I'm sure hard things happened during that time, but all I remember is how sweet my relationship with the Lord was.

It is so important to pray before you cray. When you're that close to the Lord, it's easy for Him to grab your arm before you go overboard.

When you're CLOSE to the LORD, it's easy for him TO GRAB YOUR ARM before YOU GO overboard.

Jen says own it and make it real:
Describe a time in your life where you felt as close to the Lord as I did. What is your prayer life with the Lord like? What would your anxiety look like if you developed a way of living that included the Lord in every aspect of your life? Why would it look like that?

Notes

_____

_____

_____

_____

_____

_____

_____

_____

_____

_____

_____

Perspective Paves the Way to Healing

Introductory Thoughts: The definition of perspective according to Oxford on the interwebs:

noun

1. the art of drawing solid objects on a two-dimensional surface so as to give the right impression of their height, width, depth, and position in relation to each other when viewed from a particular point. "a perspective drawing"

2. a particular attitude toward or way of regarding something; a point of view. "most guidebook history is written from the editor's perspective"

Read: Psalms 73:26; 2 Corinthians 4:17-18; Luke 5:16; Psalms 103:2; Ephesians 1:3

So, sure we can say all day "Take captive your thoughts" or "Serve others" or whatever...and all of these can and do work, but the point of this book is that sometimes you need a combination of all of these chapters or one over the other when you're deep in the muck. Anxiety is not an easy fix. There are some days that you're so stuck in the mud, you need to change your perspective to get out. **You can accomplish this in two ways: realizing how** blessed you are compared to some (others have it worse off than you) and/or changing your surroundings.

Too Blessed to Be Stressed

Sometimes we need reminding that we're too blessed to be stressed, amen? Yesterday, a friend of mine, Amanda, called me in tears while I was at the church working. She needed to come in and just emotionally vomit so she could take in a new perspective and that was fine by me. I am definitely no stranger to needing to emotionally vomit! Her week was... A LOT.

She's a single mom with two littles. Her boy had just started kindergarten four weeks ago and two days ago she had to un-enroll him due to his unacceptable behavior in the classroom. She was embarrassed and felt judged. She even reamed him a bit more than she wanted to and then felt guilty for that too!

In addition to all of this, she has a career in the mental health field where she helps clients going through all. the. things. Her heart is big and often the realities of her clients weigh her down.

Not only that, but she is also in school full time to become a nurse! Oh and let's not forget that like all of us, she is not perfect and has made mistakes in her life that have led to why she's a single mom and we all know how Satan likes to dredge up our past and throw it on us like a wet blanket, ready to suffocate us with its drenched weight when we already currently feel like we're drowning. Jerk. So, here she was.

We sat ourselves down in our church cafe and she spewed that emotional vomit while the tears flowed. I sat there kind of in awe of her. Not because I was like "Good God, woman, pull it together", but because all I was hearing was an incredibly strong and beautiful woman who was feeling a little human. She let it all out and then I smiled.

"Amanda, you are strong, beautiful and capable of way more than I could ever do. You are great with your kids, manage to pull off hours of school work and work a full time job. Your heart for your clients is big and they're lucky to have you advocating for them and praying as you go. Weeks like this always come."

I began to see her shoulders relax and she began to breathe deeply again. Her perspective began to shift and she then began to share how she realizes that given her past, things could be so much worse and for many they are. She shared that although her family struggles mentally and emotionally that at least God has given her two older women in the church that we call her "church moms". She shared that she's fully aware it's no big deal that her boy will start kindergarten the following year as many boys do that. The perspective shifts came rolling in and her heart was light again.

Changing the Scene

I also think what worked for her and what can work for you too is changing the scene. It's not often she comes to the church to chat with me, but maybe she needed to sit with a different friend or pastor than usual in a different setting rather than go home and do whatever.

For me, if I'm upset, I'll go for a walk down by the creek in my yard, or hang out in my kids' rooms for a bit. Different scenery helps your brain unlock and see things differently. It just does. Ask anyone who's ever been to Maui. If they were any kind of upset about anything in their life when their plane landed on that heavenly island, then it all immediately melted away as soon as they stepped off because you truly feel you're in paradise there. Disneyland does the same thing...for me, anyway. You just truly feel you've stepped into a world of only happiness as soon as you walk in those gates.

So, yeah...perspective paves the way to healing. Sometimes you just gotta remember what's true for you and go somewhere else to do so.

Jen says own it and make it real:

What do you believe about perspective and its relationship to healing? When in your life could you have simply changed scenery to help you get better?

Notes

_____

_____

_____

_____

_____

_____

_____

_____

_____

_____

_____

_____

Devotions at Night Make for a Good Night's Sleep

Introductory Thoughts: As someone who works to stave off anxiety, I've found that it helps to read my Bible at night. I'm too tired in the morning to be one of those awesome holy people who starts their day in the word, so that was never an option for me. I want to be awake and soak in what God has for me; not a zombie struggling to make sense of what I just read. I start my day with FB and IG. Ha!

No; for me, I end my day with Jesus. The worries of the world love to flood my heart and brain as I lay down to sleep at night and keep me awake. So, when I spend time in the word, I dream of nothing but what is lovely, pure, good and praiseworthy.

Read: 1 Chronicles 16:11; James 4:8; Psalms 1:2; Psalms 91:1; 1 John 5:14

Are you a day time Bible and devotion reader or a night time one? There is no right or wrong time. I simply wanted to make the point of sharing when my right time is because we often hear of the importance of starting your day with Jesus. I mean, geez, in my humble opinion you should start, continue AND end your day with Jesus! Jesus all day, foolz!

So, offer a prayer up to God in the morning to commit your day and then try night time reading to sleep well at night! It's just a suggestion. I have a feeling that many people who are chronically worried or sad have trouble falling and staying asleep every night. If that's you, I'm simply saying, give my method a try.

Of course, if you're one to who can't keep your eyes open as soon as you hit the pillow or your brain shuts off at a certain time of night, then this probably won't work for you. However, if you'd like to give it a shot, do it.

Why This Works For Me
Reading the Bible at night works for me because:

- **I pray as I read**. Often I use the Bible to prompt my prayers. I relate to the psalmist and pray their prayers for myself. I feel warned by the prophets and pray prayers that will direct my life, etc...
- **I gain perspective on life**. This is another way to gain perspective on the day I've just lived. As bad as my life is, I've never been thrown in a den of lions or stoned to death. Ya feel?
- **I'm reminded of the promises of God**. Jesus has overcome death. By His stripes I am healed. He'll never leave me nor forsake me. When I read my Bible, I'm reminded of His promises and that makes for a real peaceful sleep.
- **Jesus is the last thing on my mind**. What a way to end the day. Instead of all the happenings of the day reeling through my mind as I drift off into dreamland or whatever nonsense was on my Facebook feed. The king of kings, Lord of Lord and lover of my soul is on my mind. There is NO better way to go to sleep.

I remember it sometimes taking me an hour or two to fall asleep. I simply couldn't shut my brain off or get that hamster off the worry wheel. But now, since I read my Bible or whatever Jesus book I'm reading before bed, I'm often asleep within minutes of putting it down.

Let's take back sleep by picking up the Bible!

Jen says own it and make it real:
What is your bedtime routine? Why does it work or not work for you? If you were writing this chapter, what would you say is a good way for an anxious person to get a good night's sleep?

CAN'T SLEEP?
take inventory
OF THE DAY
with God.
ASK HIM:
LORD,
what was of you
&
what wasn't of you?

Notes

As Iron Sharpens Iron

Introductory Thoughts: Why I have non-anxious friends to smack some sense into me.

Read: Proverbs 27:17

Please don't get thrown off by my introductory thought. Yes, it's true that you don't just want to tell an anxious person to "get over it", but sometimes ya kinda do.

The Sometimes Exception

The sometimes exception comes into play if your 'smack some sense into ya and tell ya to get over it' friend does so with sensitivity and has invested time into graciously hearing you out in the past.

Also, I will say that although friends like this help me, they may not help you. Like I said at the beginning, I'm no expert... just a fellow fighter.

The reason friends like this bring me back to reality is because I tell myself, "If they're not worried, and I know I can trust them, then I can cool down. It's not as big of a deal as I think it is". Does that make sense? Do you see why this helps me?

It's the whole idea of "iron sharpens iron". What I lack, they provide; just as I'm sure I do for them in other areas of life and our friendship. So, when I take the liberty of emotionally vomiting on them all of my worry and sadness and fear, and they come back with a soul crushing 'come to Jesus' moment, then I know it's gonna be okay. I'm gonna be okay. Because their mind isn't in the crazy zone like mine is right now and they have my best interests at heart.

Thank God for friends who smack me right side up.

Jen says own it and make it real:
What 'iron sharpens iron' friends do you have in your life to help you when you're anxious or depressed? If you don't have any, how would you go about finding some? Why does this chapter resonate with you...or why does it not?

Notes

Doubt Your Doubts and Believe Your Beliefs

Introductory Thoughts: This is a little framed quote that I have hanging in my house that helps me a lot.

Read: James 1:6; John 20:27; Matthew 21:21

I love quotable wisdom and this one is really good for those whose thoughts run away with them. "Doubt your doubts and believe your beliefs". Come on! That's so good! Doesn't seem like doubt always comes after we were already holding a strong belief about that thing?

I know I want to be a teacher - *but I'm probably not cut out for it*

It's my dream to write a book - *but nobody will read it because it won't be any good*

I love running and I'm fast so I'm gonna do races where they splash paint or glitter on you - *others are better. I'll embarrass myself.*

I love singing. I'll try out for worship team. - *I'm too old. They'll laugh at me.*

I made the right decision with my child - *but what if I'm the worst parent ever?*

God has always been there for me. I trust him. - *but what if that was all in my head?*

It reminds me of another quote by Jeffrey R. Holland: "Doubt your doubts before you doubt your faith." Doubt is often closely entwined with emotions. Emotions are fickle. Doubt can be an indicator of something, but it doesn't mean it's indicating truth.

Take your doubt to the Lord. "God I believe, but help me in my unbelief". You know He will. "God, I'm worried, but help me with my worry". He will.

Doubt can come from stress, hurtful words others say, or delayed fruition of something you've been hoping for. When stress, hurt or delayed hope come, so does Satan with His doubt disguised as truth. Then, before you know it, we're full speed on the worry-go-round with no end in site.

Stick your leg off the side of that worry-go-round, dig your heels in and end it by repeating what you know to be true. Doubt your doubts and believe your beliefs. It's a good little quote to use as a good little tool. What did you know to be true before the doubts came? Do you have any cold hard facts to refute it? Then, doubt those doubts and believe those beliefs.

Jen says own it and make it real:
How can you doubt your doubts and believe your beliefs? Seriously. I'm looking for practical answers here. How does this quote help you if it does? What else causes doubt that I may not have listed?

DOUBT DRAGON

Notes

_____

_____

_____

_____

_____

_____

_____

_____

_____

_____

_____

Hope That Anchors the Soul

Introductory Thoughts: We won't be anxious forever. Heaven eventually comes; and THAT reality brings me comfort and peace.

Read: Hebrews 6:19; Ephesians 1:3-13

What is an anchor? An anchor is what keeps a ship stable. The crew of said ship would plunk one right down into the water to make certain that the ship stays where it's supposed to, not budging no matter what is happening in the sea around it. This is great for anxious ridden people.

What causes us to drift, anyway? Hard times, divided hearts, complacency...add that to our tendency to worry or be blue and we're lost at sea in a heartbeat.

But the good news is we're not without hope. The context of this verse comes from a promise God made to Abraham and eventually all of us. Not only did God promise this but He sealed it with an oath. All descendants of Abraham are promised every spiritual blessing in Christ.

Let's go over some of these blessings shall we? Paul says we:

- Are chosen before the world
- Are holy and blameless
- Are in His love
- Are predestined to adoption
- Are accepted
- Are redeemed

- Are forgiven
- Have his grace
- Will know His will
- Have an inheritance
- Know the truth
- Are sealed with the Holy Spirit
- Know the hope of what's ahead
- Are valuable to Him
- Have His power in us

Holy smokes! With all of that, we never have to worry! These promises are the hope that anchors the soul! Not only do we have all of this NOW, BUT we also know we'll eventually be in heaven for eternity with Him where never a fret or tear shall plague us again! I can just sit with that truth all day.

Jen says own it and make it real:
What is the hope that anchors the soul? How would you explain it to someone in your own words? How does the hope that anchors your soul help you when you're not you? What is your favorite of the spiritual blessings and why?

Notes

_____

_____

_____

_____

_____

_____

_____

_____

_____

_____

_____

_____

_____

Why Me? Well, Why Not?

I ntroductory Thoughts: It's the way of the world isn't it? When bad things happen, the default yuhquestion of all humanity is "why me"?

Read: Job 5:7

Everybody on earth, whether they struggle with anxiety or not, has had something bad happen to them, at which point they ask the expected, "Why me?" Job 5:7 tells us man is born unto trouble so there's no point in asking that question. I'm here to tell you the better question is "Why not?" Why? Because the former question will hinder you, whereas the second has the potential to set you free.

Where does asking why me place the focus? You. It places the focus on you. Take a moment to reread Chapter 1 or 3 or 4 or...a number of any others you've read so far. I believe I've made it quite clear that often the key to overcoming anxiety and depression is to focus on anyone but you.

Not only is it healthy to get your mind off yourself, but the truth of life is that bad things will always happen to you...and everyone else. Others may not struggle with anxiety but they struggle with something. It's not dumb luck or a curse. It's just life. It has nothing to do with you.

Additionally, asking "Why me?" does not offer solutions. Instead, it makes you a victim. That's the last thing you need. Asking "Why not?" allows you to start going to God. You can tell him, "I know you've placed this mountain before me, so I will not only overcome it but help others along the way". How freeing and purpose giving it is to ask, "Why not me?"

One last warning, if you're usually only anxious and not depressed, asking "Why me?" is the fast route to adding depression to your ailments. Asking "Why me?" keeps you locked in the past leaving you hopeless and depressed. Asking why not propels you forward to a mission of freedom for yourself and others.

Jen says own it and make it real:
How often do you find yourself asking "Why me"? Why is that the wrong question to ask? What other questions besides "Why not?" might be the right questions to ask?

Notes

Why Aren't *They* Anxious?

Introductory Thoughts: This one kinda goes with the last one. Obvi. But this time I'm gonna tell you why in this case you need to only worry about yourself rather than others. I know. I know. Why I gotta be so contradictory?

Read: John 21:21

Let me just be real blunt. This is not your question to ask. You are not God of the universe and you don't get to decide who struggles with what. I'm sorry that sounds harsh, but you can trust I've had to give myself the same scolding.

Like I said in the previous chapter; we all struggle with something. Struggle is a fact of life. Bad things happening are a fact of life. And hey, you don't even know for a fact whether whoever you're focusing on struggles with anxiety like you do or not. You just don't. Because once again, you're not God.

Maybe they do struggle with anxiety and don't tell anyone due to pride...or. duh...anxiety. You may feel isolated in your fight with anxiety, but rest assured once again that everybody is fighting some demon. Everybody.

Satan loves to make us feel isolated. You may feel you're the only one in the world that suffers from this in the extreme that you feel you do. Therefore you look at someone else and ask "Why not them?" You're asking that question because you're jealous. Do you seriously want to add the sin of jealousy to your plague of anxiety? Bad move.

EVERYBODY on EARTH,
whether they struggle with
anxiety, OR NOT,
has had something bad happen
to them, at which point they ask,
"Why me?"
I'M HERE TO TELL YOU THE BETTER
QUESTION IS,
"Why not?"
Why? Because the former question will
HINDER you, whereas the second has
the potential to
SET YOU FREE.

You may feel isolated in your suffering but let me be the one to tell you that sin leads to isolation as well and jealousy is definitely sin. Asking why someone doesn't suffer the way you do will only serve to make you feel even more isolated.

What you need in this moment is grace. Grace for yourself and others. Don't worry about why someone else doesn't suffer the same way you do. Bear your cross in Christ and then get up and serve them the same measure of grace that's been doled out to you.

Jen says own it and make it real:
Why does asking "Why not them?" make you jealous? How does jealousy isolate you? What are some practical things you can do right now to boot jealousy and isolation to the curb?

Jealousy Giant

Notes

_____

_____

_____

_____

_____

_____

_____

_____

_____

_____

_____

Tears Are Okay

Introductory Thoughts: Don't let them look down on you because you cry.

Read: John 11:35; Psalms 126:5; Job 16:20; Psalms 30:5; Ecclesiastes 3:4

I'm a cryer. I just am. I cry when I'm moved in a variety of directions: moved to joy, sadness, frustration...you name it. I cry during movies, commercials...I cry. It's what I do. I was once told by one of my pastors that I cry for the whole church. I'm still not sure if that's a compliment or a cut.

My uncle cries too. He said he used to be so ashamed of it that one time he prayed for God to dry his tears, and guess what? He did. God dried those tears right up. As a less than thrilling result, my uncle became a hard man. He says he began to not care about anything or anyone. His road led down a not so great path. Be careful what you pray for, people!

Then, one day he'd finally had enough. He repented. God, I'm sorry I asked you to dry my tears. I'm not ashamed anymore. I want them back. Oh, he got them back alright and returned to the man God made him to be. Soft. Easy-going. Heart of gold. Support to the weary. Mender of the broken.

Do NOT be ashamed of your tears, friend. Yes, there is wisdom in knowing how to control your tears and not let them control you. There is wisdom in knowing who is around you so you don't make them uncomfortable with too many tears. But tears mean you're passionate. Tears show you have the heart of Christ. Don't let anyone look down on you because of your tears.

Jen says own it and make it real:
Are you a crier? If so, why do you cry? Are you ashamed? Why? Does it make you uncomfortable when others cry? Why? How did my uncle's story affect you?

Notes

_____

_____

_____

_____

_____

_____

_____

_____

_____

_____

_____

Emotional Intelligence

Introductory Thoughts: When you look up the term 'emotional intelligence' on the interwebs it says, "the capacity to be aware of, control, and express one's emotions, and to handle interpersonal relationships judiciously and empathetically." Below that it says, "emotional intelligence is the key to both personal and professional success."

Read: Proverbs 29:11; Proverbs 9:7-8; Proverbs 25:20; Romans 12:16-21

As an anxious person, it's my firm belief that you need to have high emotional intelligence. Why? Because duh...it's the key to both personal and professional success. People who are not emotionally intelligent are not taken seriously. They're written off as drama queens, perpetual teenagers, and societal lepers. They're avoided like the plague. To be avoided is not good if you have anxiety or depression. So, learn how to know when to let your cray out and how much cray is too much.

How do you gain emotional intelligence and control that cray? Ah! I'm so glad you asked! There are three keys to obtaining emotional intelligence

3 Keys to Emotional Intelligence
Be Self Aware. First of all, you need self awareness. Self awareness is knowing what you tend to do, why you tend to do it AND continuing to discover what you don't know about yourself.

Knowing what you're doing is often hard because we're usually on auto-pilot. It helps to ask others how you tend to respond in situations. It also helps to carve out moments of solitude and reflect on scenarios for the sole purpose of remembering how you reacted. These moments of solitude are not for you to anxiously replay everything you think you did wrong in your mind, but to literally try to remember your body language, the words you used, and then try to understand why you went that route. Name your emotions in that moment.

Use Your Emotions for Good, Not Evil. Emotions are so useful if we direct them well and don't succumb to them. Emotions are meant to signal something to us. We need to pay attention to what our emotions are and then react properly. Be angry, but don't let it cause you to sin. Joy is good, but not if it comes from hurting someone. Fear is a good warning sign, but not if it causes you to hide in cowardice. Let your emotions guide you to what psychologists call "goal directed behaviour".

Recognize the Emotions of Others. It's important to always be paying attention to others and how they may be feeling. Once again, it's not always all about you. Realize when something is going on with someone else and be there for them in the way they need it.

Jen says own it and make it real:
How would you describe your emotional intelligence? Who is someone you trust that you can go to to help you become more self aware? I recommend a book by Terry Linhart, called The Self Aware Leader. Check it out!

Notes

Be Honest with Yourself and Others

Introductory Thoughts: Honesty is the best policy. The truth will set you free. As Ralph Waldo Emersen once said, "Truth is the property of no individual but is the treasure of all men."

Read: John 8:32

When you are anxious, or when you are anything for that matter, there can be no healing without truth. Truth comes by self awareness, considering others over yourself, rebuking lies and selfishness, trusting God, focusing on what you know to be true, holding onto your joy and keeping a right perspective...basically everything we've talked about in this book so far.

Truth sets you free! How can you heal from fear and sadness unless you find someone you trust and share your truth with them? How can you find freedom unless you're honest with yourself and God about your feelings *and* your sins?

I promise you will be locked in the grip of your anxiety prison unless you start becoming totally, completely and unashamedly honest about who you are, what you've been through, and what you've done.

DO NOT let Satan tempt you into staying quiet or believing the lies he's feeding you. I've said this many times before and I'll say it again. Condemnation leaves you hopeless whereas conviction sets you free. If you feel guilt or shame about where you find yourself and think you have to hide that, then you're experiencing condemnation. That is not of Jesus! Kick it to the curb and embrace conviction instead...because that will lead you straight into His arms.

Jen says own it and make it real:
How do you tell the difference between conviction and condemnation? What can you do to begin being honest with yourself and others today? What would you tell someone who you think is not being honest with themselves or you?

Notes

_____

_____

_____

_____

_____

_____

_____

_____

_____

_____

_____

Jesus Sweat Blood

Introductory Thoughts: Ew. Jesus sweat blood?! Is that even possible? It must be! **Jesus** was said to have been **sweating blood** before his crucifixion. Leonardo da Vinci once told about a soldier who had **bloody sweat** after battle. Hematidrosis, or hematohidrosis, is a very rare medical condition that causes you to ooze or **sweat blood** from your skin when you're not cut or injured.

Read: Luke 22:44

Think about it. This passage comes from Luke. Luke was a doctor. Luke is the only one to describe Jesus' condition as hematidrosis. Under conditions of great emotional stress, tiny capillaries in the sweat glands can rupture, thus mixing blood with perspiration. The only recorded instances of this happening to people are when they are under extreme distress.

Luke said in His *anguish* Jesus prayed and sweat this way. In His anguish. Anguish is severe mental pain or suffering. Anguish. What a strong word. If you reread chapter 12, it's no wonder He was in such anguish. To know that he was not only about to suffer physical pain but also the anguish of all victims in history as well as the evil of all sinners? Wow.

You guys, I say this all to remind you that Jesus has been where you are. You are not alone. You are not an exception. Jesus, *your* advocate, is very well aware of how you suffer. NO ONE understands more than Him. Please...when you're in anguish over anything, go to Him. He gets it. He can carry you through.

Jen says own it and make it real:

Have you ever doubted that Jesus sweat literal blood? What do you imagine that must've felt or looked like? How does knowing the anguish He was in make you feel?

Notes

_____

_____

_____

_____

_____

_____

_____

_____

_____

_____

_____

_____

Do it Afraid or Rather, Anxious

Introductory Thoughts: Surely you've heard people say, "Do it afraid". I think that's a good idea. But let's create our own anthem: "Do it anxious".

Read: Deuteronomy 20:1; 1 John 4:18; 1 Timothy 1:7; Romans 8:31; James 4:17

Fear keeps you locked in place. Frozen; unable to act. Faith helps you move forward in spite of fear. Fear seeks to torment us and steal the abundant life God has promised us. It's time to get mad, and claim our life and joy back. We are not victims! We are conquerors!

It's okay to be anxious and afraid as long as you do what you know you're to do anyway. Don't let fear and anxiety immobilize you. Fear and anxiety are not your gods. Don't bow down to them. March forward with your eyes fixed on Jesus instead of how anxious you are.

God moves on our behalf when we focus on Him instead of what makes us anxious. The feeling of fear or anxiety is simply dumb Satan trying to distract us from God and His plan for us. We may feel fear at various times in our lives but we can choose to trust God and if we need to, "Do it anxious."

In Deuteronomy 20, Israel is about to go to war. God point blank tells them to not focus on the large army or how much they have to help them. He tells them to not focus on what makes them anxious, but to focus on Him. Focus on the fact He's saved them before. Focus on the fact that he also says and is saying right now, simply go forward and I'll take care of the rest.

James 4:17 says, "So whoever knows the right thing to do and fails to do it, for him it is sin." This verse keeps me from being more afraid of anxiety and the what ifs than God. I may be scared to do what's being asked of me, but my fear of being separated from God is greater. I choose to follow Him.

Jen says own it and make it real:
Describe some times you were immobilized by anxiety. What was the outcome of that? Describe a time you "did it anxious". What was the outcome of that? How can you begin to do it anxious? How can you help others do it anxious?

DO it ANXIOUS

Notes

Hugs Not Drugs

Introductory Thoughts: This title needs to be on a t-shirt. They probably make these. Somebody buy me one.

Read: Ephesians 5:18; 1 Peter 5:8-9

The point of this chapter is simply to say don't rely solely on medication to heal your anxiety. Yes, I said above that I use Prozac and that's okay. It's okay because it's not my only source of help and support. Everything I've written in this book thus far are tools I use to help me stay above the waves. Please remember that medications are just a tool to partner with Jesus.

I don't even know most of you reading this book but I know that I love you. I know that I love the person God envisioned when He created you. I know I love the purpose you have and the part you're to play in this game called life. I know that if you weren't completely you, but an altered you, due to drugs and alcohol, it would be a tragedy.

Alcohol. Yes. I just said drugs *and* alcohol. I'm not one of those crazy Christians dead set against alcohol. I don't believe drinking is a sin...necessarily. Here's my thoughts on alcohol:

- Very few people solely use it socially (New Year's Eve, etc)
- Very few people use it for health (heart, health etc)
- Very few people can stop after one or two
- Very few people can drink in a crowd and not cause someone to stumble

- Very few people can keep it off social media in order to not cause someone to stumble
- Very few people gain anything worthwhile from it

Very few. Here's what else I think:

- Most people are not their most genuine and unique self when affected by drugs and alcohol.

Use wisdom and moderation. Keep your head clear. Keep your mind and body healthy. Choose people and God over meds...or with very little meds...or only meds for a time. Whatever works for you. Hugs not drugs.

Jen says own it and make it real:
What do you imagine it's like to be drunk or wasted? Have you been? Were you your best self in that moment? Why might drugs/alcohol be a good idea for anxiety (yes I said good)? Have you seen friends or family who self medicate or legit medicate and it changed who they were? What are your thoughts on all of this?

Notes

_____

_____

_____

_____

_____

_____

_____

_____

_____

_____

_____

_____

All Kinds of Anxious

I ntroductory Thoughts: There are so many varieties of anxiety. Which one(s) are you?

Read: Psalms 94:19

Generalized Anxiety Disorder, sometimes referred to as GAD, is characterized by chronic anxiety, ridiculous worry and stress, even when there is little or nothing "wrong".

Obsessive-Compulsive Disorder (OCD) or CDO (that's a joke...see what I did there?) is characterized by recurrent, unwanted thoughts (obsessions) and/or repetitive behaviors (compulsions). I tend to count things obsessively: telephone poles when driving, buttons on a person's outfit when they're preaching or speaking, tiles on ceilings. I'm a counter. I also have rituals...cleaning has to be done an exact certain way. My hands have to be washed an exact certain way. I'm weird, man.

Panic Disorder is characterized by unexpected and repeated episodes of a crazy amount of fear accompanied by physical symptoms like chest pain, heart flutters, shortness of breath, dizziness, or tummy aches.

Post-Traumatic Stress Disorder (PTSD) is an anxiety disorder that can develop after exposure to a terrifying event or experience. This is what you hear our amazing military people go through a lot in history. However, I've also had a friend be diagnosed with it due to not being able to nurse her first baby.

Social Phobia (or Social Anxiety Disorder) is an anxiety disorder where one has overwhelming anxiety and excessive self-consciousness in simple social situations. Social phobia can be one or more of the following: fear of speaking in front of others, eating or drinking in front of others or simply truly experiencing symptoms almost anytime they are around anyone.

Jen says own it and make it real:
Professionally diagnosed or not, which ones do you relate to? How does it make you feel seeing the various orders defined?

Notes

_____

_____

_____

_____

_____

_____

_____

_____

_____

_____

_____

_____

Today I'm Fine

Introductory Thoughts: Today I'm fine, but what about to-morrow?! I could be anxious tomorrow and now I'm anx-ious about being anxious!

Read: Romans 8:38-39; Jeremiah 17:7-8; Phillippians 4:6-7; John 14:27

Haha. It's so funny, but it's so true. Even when us anxious people are fine, we're anxious about the anxiety coming back! Let me tell you a story.

Yesterday, after dropping my 6th grader at school, I passed out while driving and crashed. It's October and it's a big month for me. Tonight I'm meeting the comedian that graces the cover of my first book and was the first one to endorse it for me. Next weekend, I'm speaking at my very first conference! I've done re-treats and events but never a conference! It's so exciting. The next weekend after that I'm flying to Ohio, as my first book, As My Mind Unwinds, is a top 10 finalist for a book award and I'm hoping to win! The last weekend of the month going into Novem-ber, I'm helping an amazing team put together a conference. In the midst of it all, my family is going through a lot due to a recent move following a death in our family, I recently got promoted at work, I'm trying to finish this book and SO MUCH MORE.

So, back to that crash. I was driving home after dropping off my son and I thought I was getting pink eye. I was so ticked about it because I had to meet my comedian friend and everything else and could NOT GET SICK. All of the sudden I felt like I was gonna pass out and sure enough...next thing I know, I'm waking up to an off duty fire-fighter asking if I'm okay and what my name is...all while I'm hanging upside down strapped into my seatbelt.

They say I must've been stressed or anxious.

Are you kidding me?! Anxiety controls my driving now?! No. No it does not. My immediate thoughts were I can never drive again and I absolutely refuse to drive my kids anywhere because I can't be trusted to stay conscious.

I'm fine today. I'm conscious today...but what about tomorrow? What if anxiety takes the wheel again? What if I pass out at the worst time again? What if?

Friends, I can't live in the what ifs. I'm gonna take what happened, use the wisdom of my doctors, myself and Jesus to try to keep it from happening again and then, I'm gonna get behind the wheel. My confidence is in God and I refuse to be anxious, but instead I'll bring my anxiety to Him with a grateful heart for all He's done. I refuse to worry about tomorrow. Today has enough trouble of its own and I got stuff to get done, son!

Jen says own it and make it real:
How are you anxious about being anxious? What would you tell someone who is anxious about anxiety? What would you tell you? How does being anxious about being anxious make you feel? What are you gonna do about it?

Notes

How Do People Cope Without Jesus?

Introductory Thoughts: I often think about what all of humanity struggles with day in and day out and honestly wonder, how the heck to people make it without Jesus?!

Read: Colossians 3:15; 2 Thessalonians 3:16; Psalms 55:22; Psalms 23:4; Psalms 56:3

I haven't been through as much as some, but I've experienced life. When my first son was born, I believe he or I might have died if not for the amazing invention of c-sections. My brother died in a tragic way and I still don't know all the truth behind what happened. I lost my best friend in life because she admitted she wanted a more surface level friendship, not just with me but with anyone in her life. I had a car accident from fainting behind the wheel!

Life is incredibly hard. A lot of it makes no sense. I often feel dazed and confused but at least I have Jesus! The only reason I ever leave my house or that I haven't committed suicide is because of Jesus. The only reason I remain in my right mind even after periods of feeling crazy is Jesus! The only reason I can make any relationship in my life work is because of Jesus! The answer is always Jesus! The answer to anything life has thrown at anyone has always been and is always gonna be Jesus.

Jesus is THE way, THE truth and THE life. He came so that you may have life and have it to the fullest. If you've read to this point of this book and are still not certain you have Jesus. Reach out and take hold now.

Jen says own it and make it real:

Pray with me: "Lord, it IS impossible to make it without you. I need you. I've failed but you have not. You died to set me free and I have faith in that. Please come into my life and take over. Forgive me for trying to go it alone. In Jesus' name, AMEN."

Notes

_____

_____

_____

_____

_____

_____

_____

_____

_____

_____

_____

_____